Original title:
Violets of Verse

Copyright © 2025 Creative Arts Management OÜ
All rights reserved.

Author: Ronan Whitfield
ISBN HARDBACK: 978-1-80567-008-7
ISBN PAPERBACK: 978-1-80567-088-9

Soliloquies of the Summer

The grasshoppers dance with flair,
Their leggy moves beyond compare.
A sunburnt nose and ice cream splat,
Who knew fun could look like that?

The daisies whisper silly jokes,
While bees hum tunes with buzzing folk.
Silly squirrels plot their next snack,
In this warm weather, who needs a nap?

The Blooming Quatrain

In gardens bright, the gnomes conspire,
With toadstool hats and eyes of fire.
They plot to steal the sun's warm rays,
Yet sleep through half of sunny days.

While flowers giggle, petals sway,
The bugs all strut in wild array.
A mismatched shoe makes fashion bold,
In summer tales yet to be told.

Vignettes in the Vegetation

The tomatoes wear a crown of green,
With splashes of red, they steal the scene.
A cucumber jokes about its length,
While squash shows off its hidden strength.

With laughter rising from the beans,
And jokes about their fiber scenes,
The veggies cheer, they won't be beat,
In this amusing, sunny seat.

Verse Under the Violet Sky

Beneath the clouds that skip and hop,
A kite flies high while children flop.
With giggles echoing near and far,
They giggle at their flying star.

In twilight hues, the stars appear,
But fireflies outshine without fear.
As nature whispers tales of old,
The nights are funny, bright, and bold.

Inked Flora

With petals brushed by ink so bright,
A doodle flower takes to flight.
It giggles when the raindrops fall,
And dances with the breeze, so small.

In sketchbook pages, it does thrive,
A colorful jester, so alive.
Each line a tale, each curve a laugh,
A masterpiece of nature's craft.

When bees arrive for cheeky chats,
They trade sweet secrets with the cats.
The gardener chuckles, what a sight,
As blooms become the jokes of night.

So here's to flora, inked with cheer,
A giggling garden that we hold dear.
With every leaf, let laughter grow,
In this bright patch, joy's sure to flow.

Shadows of the Garden

In shadows lurk the flowers shy,
They stifle giggles, oh my, oh my!
Behind the leaves, they whisper low,
Secret jokes that only they know.

A daisy trips on a stalk,
And peonies begin to squawk.
As sunbeams peek through leafy smiles,
The garden bursts with laugh-filled miles.

The tulips tease the passing bees,
"Hurry up, don't catch a sneeze!"
A butterfly rolls with laughter loud,
Joining the giggles, feeling proud.

Under the moon, the whispers grow,
A raucous play of flora's show.
The shadows dance, the laughter blooms,
In a garden brimming with silly rooms.

The Romantic Thicket

In thickets thick, a lovebird's song,
Wobbles sweetly, not for long.
A tangled vine, it holds a tale,
Of shy petunias that laugh and wail.

With flowers puffed with pride so tall,
They flirt with sunbeams, can't help but sprawl.
A bumblebee, with wings so bold,
Whispers sweet nothings, stories told.

Yet, roses blush when daisies tease,
"Keep it classy beside the trees!"
Amid this thicket, hearts collide,
Chasing laughter through flowery tide.

A playful dance, a spin of fate,
Where love and giggles celebrate.
In this romantic, tangled space,
Flora finds its funny grace.

Harmonies of the Hearth

In gardens green, where laughter blooms,
The hearth sings sweetly, chasing glooms.
With pots of soil, we plant the cheer,
And green-thumbed glee fills the sphere.

The pansies jive with daffodils,
They shake their heads, they've got the skills!
A serenade of roots and leaves,
Compose a tune that never grieves.

The veggies join in on the fun,
"Hey, lettuce party, oh what a run!"
As sweet tomatoes roll and laugh,
In nature's kitchen, a funny half.

So gather 'round this garden stage,
Where every plant can laugh and gauge.
In harmonies both bright and rare,
The hearth hums joy for all to share.

Palettes of Emotion

In a world of colors bright,
The crayons start a silly fight.
Red claimed love, while blue just cried,
Green said, "Juice!" as it slipped and slid.

Yellow laughed, a sunlit jest,
While purple danced, it did its best.
The painter smirked, with brush in hand,
Now chaos reigns, just as he planned.

Castles in the Clover

We built our dreams on blades so green,
With marshmallow towers — a sweet scene!
But ants marched in, so bold and sly,
Claiming the castle, "We'll occupy!"

The king was crowned with a flower hat,
While chatting squirrels all sat and spat.
A royal decree — let's have some snacks!
Flavorful crumbs from our lunch packs!

A Stroll Through Strophes

A poet walked on rhymes so bold,
Tripping on metaphors, truth be told.
Each step a giggle, a line so quick,
"Hey! Watch my verse!" — it did a kick.

But lo and behold, a pun appeared,
With laughter sprouting, it silently sneered.
"You're writing nonsense, that's not a feat!"
Yet the poet retorts, "But isn't it sweet?"

The Singing Garden

In the garden where flowers sway,
Each petal sings its own bouquet.
Daisies shout, 'We're the happiest here!'
While roses blush, overcome by cheer.

The daisies danced a jig so spry,
As bumblebees buzzed, oh my, oh my!
Laughter echoed through leafy greens,
As weeds joined in — the funniest scenes!

The Ink of Iris

In a garden where laughter blooms,
Pens twirl like playful brooms.
Words dance under the sun's bright glare,
With ink that spills without a care.

Bees laugh with a buzzing sound,
As rhymes tumble all around.
A butterfly winks and takes a flight,
Chasing verses into the night.

Papers rustle as jokes unfold,
Each line more daring, or so we're told.
With every stroke, we draw a grin,
As the scribbles turn into a din.

So let's ink our stories, silly and spry,
Where lines can giggle and rhymes can fly.
With each quirky twist, life's a fun spree,
In the realm of ink, we're all so free.

Blue Shadows of Inspiration

Under clouds of cotton candy hue,
Ideas pirate ships, sailing from view.
With giggles echoing against the sky,
Inspiration's shadow flits and flies.

A whimsical thought, a silly plot,
Sprouting wings in the sunny spot.
With each turn of phrase, a chuckle is spun,
Crafting chaos—oh what fun!

The shadows pitch a playful game,
Why be serious? It's all the same.
Let's dance with muses, cheeky and bright,
As laughter sprinkles the cool twilight.

So dive into the blue, my friend,
Where the shades of mirth never end.
With each inkblot, happily lose track,
In these shadows, we'll never look back.

Rhymes Wrapped in Floral Folds

Petals whisper secrets side by side,
As thoughts flit on a cheeky ride.
Wrapped in laughter, tied with twine,
Each verse a bouquet, wildly divine.

Daisies giggle, roses make bets,
While the poppies boast funny debts.
Every line a curl, a playful twist,
Growing rhymes too good to resist.

With stems that sway to this playful tune,
And laughter rising like a balloon.
We gather words in a flowery box,
As quirky phrases soar like flocks.

So frolic through this poetic glade,
Where fun is the secret that won't fade.
Each floral fold has a story to tell,
In a garden of giggles, all is well.

The Essence of Evening Primrose

In the dusk's embrace, where giggles dwell,
Evening blooms with stories to tell.
Primrose paints the horizon bright,
As words frolic in the fading light.

A sprinkle of humor, a dash of charm,
In this garden, all feelings are warm.
With each petal, we toss a line,
Crafting tales that taste like wine.

The night hums with a whimsical grin,
As each verse joins in, inviting a spin.
With laughter echoing 'neath the stars,
Our poetic hearts dance like guitars.

So raise a toast to the evening's grace,
Where humor and rhyme find their place.
Under the soft glow of twilight's dream,
We'll spin the essence, let laughter beam.

Stanzas Softly Blooming

In fields of purple, tales unfold,
Jokes wrapped in memories spun from gold.
Each bloom holds secrets, fresh and bright,
Painted with laughter, day and night.

A lavender laughter drifts in air,
Where rhymes and punchlines bloom with flair.
Tickled tulips wiggle with delight,
In this garden where humor takes flight.

Whispers of Lavender

In the garden, plants do chatter,
One thinks it's mad, but what's the matter?
A daffodil slips and calls it a crime,
While the daisies giggle, lost in their thyme.

A bee buzzes, wearing tiny specs,
Accusing the flowers of bad syntax wrecks.
They bloom in colors, absurd and bright,
Debating the rules of a leaf-lettered fight.

The sun winks down, with a cheeky glow,
"Don't quit your day jobs," it seems to bestow.
A rose blushes deeply, "I'm more than my hue!"
"Just petal-tastic," retorts sweet pea with a view.

So the green gang jives under skies of blue,
Spilling their secrets, who knew they could dew?
A laugh in the leaves, a pun in the breeze,
They jest until twilight, at ease, with such tease.

Garden of Unspoken Lines

In the shadows where the daisies plot,
Grow dreams of wild hues, quite a hot spot.
Chickens peck softly, in vain to relate,
The poetic chaos ignites the debate.

A cactus wants in on the querulous chat,
"Stop prickling me here, really, how rude is that?"
The lilies just snicker, taking care to bloom,
In tones of green giggles, clearing the gloom.

With butterflies hatching their gossip-filled wings,
They dance in the sunlight, spreading the springs.
"Where art thou, lilac?" they tease with a grin,
Sweeter than nectar with mischief within.

Each fragrance a sonnet, each color a jest,
In a garden of whispers, the friendly fest.
So while daylight holds court, do take a glance,
At this merriment garden where all plants dance.

Twilight Blooms

As night descends on the fidgety tulips,
The owls take bets on the plant's funny quips.
"Do roses wear lipstick?" one wise scribe calls,
The petals shake their heads, try not to fall.

The moon's reflection stirs giggles galore,
Cacti compete for the tallest folklore.
"Your spikes aren't that charming," chirps mint with a grin,
"Just chill with the jokes, let the night begin!"

A rogue petunia dons shades of delight,
Proposing a dance-off under soft light.
With each little twirl, they trip on the bark,
"Keep it real, ferns, stop embarrassing the park!"

Their laughter floats high, mingling with the breeze,
Plant personas alive, planting their tease.
As darkness envelopes, pranks stir and loom,
Forever the fun in the twilight blooms.

Serenade in Shades

In the garden, a riot of colors abound,
Fruits of laughter like music profound.
"Is that pumpkin orange, or confused lemon yellow?"
Their tunes twist and turn, each pitch a fun-fellow.

A whispering breeze plays the serenade,
To tulips with secrets in every charade.
"Can daisies be jazz?" croons a bold violette,
"It's more of a swing, you just haven't felt yet!"

Bumblebees tapping, like percussion divine,
Compare pollen-rich verses, sipping on wine.
"Note to self," says a petal, "always show flair;"
While a shy peony hides, but breathes in the air.

In the symphony's light, who knows what they'll find?
A bouquet of giggles, sweet scents intertwined.
So sway with the evening, let joy dictate,
In shades of delight, together they create.

Musings Among the Marigolds

In gardens bright with yellow cheer,
The marigolds are loud and clear.
They dance around in silly hats,
And gossip like a bunch of cats.

They hold a tea with daisies too,
While sipping mint and wishing blue.
A sunflower spills all the tea,
And laughs, "I'm taller, look at me!"

A bumblebee joins in the jest,
With jokes that put the blooms to rest.
They chuckle soft, then burst with glee,
As petals fall like confetti.

But in this lively floral spree,
The lilies just roll eyes in glee.
They're sniffing scents of fancy fakes,
And giggling at the silly makes.

Fluid Fragrance

In fragrant fields where scents do play,
The roses blush, the stinks decay.
A daisy dons a big red nose,
While hyacinths just strike a pose.

Beneath a tree where blooms collide,
Theurs indistinct, like joke confides.
A lilac whispers, "What a smell!"
As geraniums burst out in yell.

The lavender sings, "I'm quite the catch!"
While petals clash in floral match.
They swear that pollen makes them wise,
Yet sneezy jokes are their disguise.

In every breeze, a giggle flows,
As blooms erupt in chaos shows.
Amidst the fun and fragrance clear,
Laughter surrounds like bubbles, dear.

Verse in Full Bloom

A daffodil dons sunglasses bright,
And claims it's got a stunning sight.
It fluffs its petals, strikes a pose,
While tulips giggle, rhyming woes.

Old roses start a rap so grand,
While violets play in flower band.
They burst with rhymes, a silly mix,
And toss in puns like flower tricks.

The daisies roll their eyes, it's clear,
They think the show is just too dear.
But join the crowd, they can't resist,
As dandelions shout, they softly twist.

And in this garden, laughter blooms,
As nature paints with all her hues.
The verse is fun, no need for gloom,
In petals bright, we all find room.

The Color of Emotion

A petunia sighs, "Life's a race!"
While snapdragons wear a frowning face.
The colors clash, a wild spree,
As blossoms dance in jubilee!

A buttercup mocks the busy bees,
And tosses pollen in the breeze.
With every bloom, a tale is spun,
In vibrant hue, they just have fun.

In swirling shades of laughs and sighs,
The colors wink, they flirt, they rise.
A rainbow caught in garden tease,
As frustration wilts among the leaves.

Oh, how the flowers love to play,
With hues that brighten up the day.
In this bouquet of joyous cheer,
Emotions weave, so crystal clear!

Fields of Rhyme

In fields where silly stanzas grow,
The flowers bloom with laughter's glow.
Each petal sprinkles puns around,
A garden where pure jest is found.

With bumblebees that dance and hum,
They tickle blooms with every thrum.
Why did the daffodil wear a hat?
To cover up its bud of fat!

The daisies giggle in the breeze,
While tulips try to make a tease.
The roses crack a joke or two,
And lilies laugh until they're blue.

So gather 'round and share a laugh,
With every verse a little gaff.
In fields of rhyme where joy's the rule,
A witty thought is always cool!

Blossoms and Ballads

In gardens lush with tunes so bright,
The blossoms sing from morn till night.
With every note, a wacky twist,
A ballad blooms that can't be missed.

The marigolds wear socks so bold,
While sunflowers tell tales of old.
They prance around in quirky glee,
As daisies nod, "Oh, let it be!"

A rose declared, "I'll write a song,
A funny one, it won't be long!"
And every note that floated free,
Had the bees buzzing in harmony.

So join the dance, let laughter flow,
With every rhyme, let giggles grow.
In fields of bloom and playful tunes,
We sway beneath the laughing moons!

Nature's Lyric

Amidst the rustling leaves so green,
Nature's jesters often preen.
With every laugh the trees do share,
They tickle winds that brush the air.

The squirrels gather for a show,
To act out scenes of high and low.
A nut drops down, a fumble quick,
"Oh dear, was that my acorn trick?"

The brook is bubbling with delight,
As frogs jump in, a splashy sight.
"Why did the lily cross the stream?
To meet her friends and build a dream!"

So listen close to nature's call,
With every giggle, you'll stand tall.
In this grand tale of fun and cheer,
With Nature's lyric, joy is near!

The Inked Garden

In an inked garden, words take flight,
With scribbles dancing, oh what a sight!
Each line a sprout, so bold and bright,
Where laughter grows, day turns to night.

The quill-nib birds sing tales of fun,
As sunlit verses play and run.
"Why did the paper refuse to play?
Because it knew it had a rough day!"

The inkpots spill with giggles sweet,
As stanza buds sprout on repeat.
A ribbon tied around the bloom,
Proclaims the joy that fills the room.

So dip your brush in colors grand,
And paint a world like no one can.
In this inked garden, let's unite,
Where every word brings pure delight!

Stanzas in Bloom

In a garden of giggles, the flowers do chatter,
A daisy told secrets, his gossip, a platter.
With each little bloom, a jest in the air,
Petals are tickling, laying laughter bare.

Bumblebees buzzing, they dance through the sun,
Chasing after each other, oh, what silly fun!
The daisies all chuckle, their heads nodding wide,
A tulip in tights just can't hide his pride.

The lilies are laughing, all dressed up in white,
While the roses play pranks, oh what a delight!
Each bloom is a jester, on nature's grand stage,
In this frolicsome garden, the flowers engage.

So join in the laughter, come sip on the dew,
With petals a-flutter, there's joy waiting for you!
In this world of nonsense, let worries take flight,
For in every petal, there's pure, playful light.

Secrets of the Violet Sky

Under skies of purple, the clouds wear a grin,
Whispers of humor that dance on the wind.
Raindrops are giggling, they splash on the ground,
As butterflies, fluttering, spin round and round.

A star fell last Tuesday, it laughed on its way,
Telling the moon how to brighten the day.
While shadows were stargazing, the sun played a tune,
The whole sky erupted in giggles by noon.

The dawn wore a bowtie, the dusk tried a hat,
Colors in chaos, not caring for that.
Jokes were exchanged in a hue of delight,
As everyone danced 'neath the twinkling starlight.

So cherish the laughter that skies can bestow,
Where secrets are shared and good humor can grow.
In the cosmos of whimsy, we all have a part,
Creating a tapestry spun from the heart.

A Palette of Petals

Colors collide in a pot of bright hues,
Petals are mixing like artists with booze.
The roses are red, but they painted them blue,
While daisies in polka dots shout, "Look at me too!"

A sunflower winked at a nearby geranium,
"Let's form a band; we'll call it Petalium!"
With a beat made of breezes, they played with delight,
Each flower nodding to the rhythm of light.

An orchid told puns, they landed like bricks,
While tulips were giggling and counting their tricks.
In this wild garden, where laughter's the brush,
Each petal's a canvas, come join in the rush!

So pick up your paintbrush, let colors ignite,
In the joy of creation, let's share in the light.
With petals a-popping, creativity's high,
In this palette of laughter, let's laugh until dry.

Rhythms Among the Roses

In the heart of the garden, where rhythms are found,
The roses are dancing to a jazzy sound.
With petals a-swirling, they glide on their stems,
While bees beat the drums with their buzzing emblems.

A lily in stripes said, "I'm ready to groove!"
The daisies chimed in, "Let's all make a move!"
With vines intertwined, they twirled round and round,
In this floral fiesta, pure joy knows no bounds.

The orchids are swinging, with laughter they sway,
Each bloom getting dizzy, they dance through the day.
The colors are vibrant, a melody sweet,
As flowers unite in this whimsical beat.

So come join the chorus, let flowers take flight,
In the rhythms of nature, where laughter's the light.
Among all the roses, a symphony's spun,
In this garden of giggles, let's dance and have fun!

Pollen of Dreams

In fields of thought, where daisies laugh,
I trip on rhymes, each word a gaffe.
Bees buzz with jokes, sweet nectar's shared,
In the garden of wit, how we've fared!

Tall tales sprout from whispered breeze,
Tickles and giggles among the leaves.
Petals prance in a silly dance,
Chasing shadows, they take a chance!

But in the night, when stars ignite,
Dreams take flight like a kite in sight.
With every tickle, a story blooms,
A patch of laughter in brightest rooms.

So here we stand, in this silly spree,
Crafting puns under the jolly tree.
May the pollen swirl, let it abide,
In the laughter-filled meadow, let joy reside!

Bouquet of Lines

A bunch of words, all tied in twine,
A sassy sentence, oh how divine!
They giggle and wiggle in pots galore,
Who knew phrases could be such a chore?

A pun in the petals, a jest in the stem,
Each line like a bloom, a botanical gem.
Swirling and twirling in bright, funny hues,
Making each reader feel light with the blues.

With laughter as sunshine, they wiggle so bold,
Stories unfold like the finest of gold.
Buds bursting with joy, each one a surprise,
Check out the bouquet, it's quite the prize!

So gather your thoughts and let them entwine,
In a bustling garden, a bouquet of lines.
For laughter will sprout, amidst words that tease,
Come join the fun, and take a big sneeze!

Fables in the Ferns

Amongst the fronds, tales take their stand,
With giggling leaves, they make demands.
Fables abound, with a cheeky grin,
Come, join this ride, let the fun begin!

Squirrels recount tales of whacky pursuits,
While rabbits debate their fashionable suits.
Each whispering fern has a saga to tell,
Of wacky adventures that promise to swell.

A wise old owl, with spectacles tight,
Shares quirky fables from morn until night.
Legends so funny, they leave you in stitches,
As laughter cascades from the wild, leafy niches.

So venture with glee through the lush, green trails,
For fables in ferns are like wind in the sails.
Let stories entwine with chirps and with cheers,
Creating a symphony that tickles your ears!

Flowery Prose

In gardens of prose, where the words bloom free,
Each sentence a blossom, a bright jubilee.
With petals like giggles that float on the breeze,
Words dance and twirl with enchanting ease.

The sunbeams laugh, warming up the page,
As metaphors play in a whimsical cage.
Adjectives flutter like butterflies bold,
Painting bright hues in stories retold.

Each paragraph bursts like a garden in spring,
With humor that bubbles, oh how it can sing!
A splash of delight in each flowered insight,
Crafting prose that feels airy and light.

So come take a stroll where the flowers compose,
Join the merry dance in this flowery prose.
For laughter and joy are the colors we seek,
In the blooming of words, let us all peek!

Verses at Dawn

At dawn, the birds all sing,
But they can't find their bling!
A squirrel swings from tree to tree,
Chasing acorns, wild and free.

The coffee pot begins to boil,
As I wrestle with the foil!
Pancakes stacked as towers stand,
And syrup's flowing like a band.

The Whispering Thymes

In the garden, herbs do chatter,
Their secrets spill, then splatter!
The basil tickles thyme's green ear,
While rosemary just rolls in fear.

Mint does dance a spry old jig,
Sage complains it's now too big!
Oregano starts playing tunes,
As they duel with silly spoons.

Cascade of Color

A splash of paint, a brush in hand,
Each stroke seems so unplanned!
The canvas laughs, it can't decide,
What colors live, what colors hide.

A purple splash, a dreadful blot,
Is this a flower? No, it's not!
Yet chaos blooms in fun delight,
As rainbows emerge, oh what a sight!

Rhyme and Roses

Roses are red, so they profess,
While violets laugh at the dress!
Tulips strut, all bold and bright,
They're competing in this flower fight.

A daisy giggles, in the mix,
Challenging petals to some tricks!
Geraniums join, with a twist of fate,
In this bloom of fun and playful state!

Rhapsody of Rare Petals

In a garden full of blooms,
Where daisies wear their plumes,
A pickle jar, it took a dive,
The flowers laughed, oh how they jive!

With petals bright and leaves so bold,
They plot to steal some sugar gold,
A bee nearby, it caught the scene,
And buzzed along, a happy queen!

The roses rolled in laughter's thrall,
As tulips tried to do a crawl,
But when a breeze began to blow,
They all fell down, oh what a show!

So if you wander through this place,
Don't miss the flowers' funny grace,
For laughter blooms in sunny air,
In every petal, love and flair!

Tapestry of Tansies

Tansies in a row they stand,
With petals painted by the hand,
They dance to tunes, oh what a sight,
With giggles floating, pure delight!

A whimsied critter hops so near,
He steals a snack, the flowers cheer,
They whisper tales of clumsy winks,
As raindrops drip, the garden thinks!

One stem wears shoes, a fancy pair,
While others toss their blossoms fair,
The bumblebees do join the fun,
A buzzing squad, oh what a run!

In this tapestry of cheer,
Each color laughs, so crystal clear,
With blooms and smiles, the day is bright,
A garden party, pure delight!

Petal-Soft Verses

Petal-soft, the whispers flow,
Each flower laughs, a little show,
They tell the tales of silly nights,
With moonbeams dancing in their sights!

A fox in shades of purple hue,
Pretends to hide, yet all can view,
He trips and falls upon the ground,
While daisies giggle all around!

With nectar sips and pollen fun,
They host a race beneath the sun,
The bumblebees just can't keep up,
While ladybugs play hopscotch—yup!

In every petal, tales unfold,
With ecstasy, the flowers bold,
For nature smiles with every jest,
And blooms their stories, simply blessed!

Harmonies in Hidden Gardens

In hidden gardens where flowers meet,
They sing of hiccups, oh so sweet,
With rustling leaves and giggly glee,
They share the tales of bumblebee!

A sunflower tried to steal a hat,
But on a bubble, off he sat,
He spun around, a sight to see,
While pansies rolled in pure debris!

The daisies danced in awkward lines,
And burst into their silly signs,
With petals flapping like old flags,
Their laughter rang, no need for rags!

So wander through this joyful place,
And join the blooms in merry chase,
For in their hearts, a symphony,
Awaits to share the joy of free!

Petals of Poetry

A flower danced on rhymes so tight,
Its petals told jokes, what a sight!
With giggles and chuckles, they bloomed with glee,
Whispering verses to the buzzing bee.

In a garden of quips, a bloom outshone,
Crafting sonnets from seeds it had sown.
A pun here, a jest, it jiggled with grace,
Leaving fellow flowers rolling in place.

Roses rolled eyes at the daffodils' glee,
"Not another limerick!" they cried with a plea.
But the petals kept spilling their laughs in the air,
Who knew that such blooms could be so debonair?

So remember, dear poets, with laughter's embrace,
Even blossoms can find their own funny place.
In the tale of the garden, let humor show rise,
For petals of laughter are the best kind of prize.

Ink and Flora

Ink spilled on petals, a glorious mess,
Sketching the antics of nature's finesse.
A daisy wore glasses, its style quite bold,
While the tulips debated if weather turned cold.

With vines twisting tales of mischief and fun,
The roses chimed in, "Oh, we're the ones!"
Tickled by breezes that whispered of cheer,
They plotted their pranks, so silly and clear.

A daffodil's joke left the daisies in tears,
"C'mon, you know that's not how it appears!"
Yet laughter rang out 'neath the sun's warm embrace,
Even cacti cracked smiles at this happy place.

So let ink flow free with the scent of the blooms,
For poems sprout laughter in all of our rooms.
In this garden of whimsy, we'll twirl with delight,
Where flora and humor are eternally bright.

The Language of Lilacs

Oh lilacs, you jokers with petals so grand,
Spoke secrets and giggles with each little stand.
A purple one winked, 'There's no need to sigh,
For words can be funny, just give them a try!'

They tickled the sounds of the wandering breeze,
With rhymes that could bring the most stiff to their knees.

"Who knew flowers could rhyme?" asked the hapless bee,

As the lilacs erupted in fits of glee.

A joke was exchanged with each wave of a stem,
Leaving tulips convinced they were better than them.
"Dare to challenge our flair?" a lilac would tease,
"To your wit, we'll respond with whimsical ease!"

In this language of laughter, let blossoms be wise,
For petals that giggle are the heart's true prize.
So dance with the lilacs, let joy fill the air,
In the garden of humor, there's magic to share.

Echoes in the Meadow

In the meadow of chuckles, a chorus arose,
From daisies to daisies, the laughter just glows.
Echoes of jest in the sweet summer air,
Where each flowering friend had a tale to share.

A poppy trumpeted, "Hey, step right up!
I'll tell you a joke about a hiccupping cup!"
The rest stood in stitches, their petals askew,
With giggles that burst as the fun only grew.

The grass blades chimed in, "We can rhyme as well!
A pun on our height? Oh, what a swell sell!"
So they made up a story, all lush and so bright,
Of flowers who flourished with humor and light.

So wander through meadows where joy yields its grace,
In echoes of laughter, find your own place.
For every good pun and sweet giggle you hear,
Is a bloom celebrating the joy of being near.

The Color Wheel of Thought

In a garden of colorful dreams,
The sun plays tricks and it gleams.
Blue is for laughter, green is for glee,
Yellow's for snacks, yes that's the key.

Reds bloom like jokes in a crowd,
Tickling fancies, slightly loud.
Orange whispers, 'Come take a ride!'
While purple giggles, 'There's nothing to hide!'

With petals bright, the thoughts take flight,
Under the moon, dancing with light.
Each hue a chuckle, a wink, a tease,
In this bloom is pure joy, if you please.

So let your mind spin like a top,
With colors that bounce and never stop.
In this painted patch, we find our cheer,
Flowering thoughts that all hold dear.

A Symphony of Stems

Amongst the stems, a band does play,
With leafy notes that sway and sway.
The trumpet's a tulip, bold and bright,
And daisies drum, oh, what a sight!

The violins are in perfect tune,
Swaying gently in the afternoon.
A carrot on bass, with rhythm so ripe,
This green orchestra, what a hype!

As petals twirl, they dance around,
In this garden-stage, laughter's found.
A crescendo of giggles, a flurry of fun,
In the symphony, no one's outdone.

So grab a flower, join in the sound,
Let the melody in petals abound.
For joy is the song in this leafy show,
In every note a funny flow.

Rhapsody in Petals

In a meadow where giggles arise,
Petals swirl like quirky pies.
Each color a giggle, each shape a grin,
Where the sun's rays invite a lively spin.

Buttercups tease with their sunny glee,
As roses blush, then wink, you see.
A daffodil sings with a voice so bright,
Turning every moment into pure light.

Tulips whisper secrets with flair,
Tickling the breeze, as they dance in air.
A rhapsody hums in the bloom-filled embrace,
Every petal's a note in this joyous place.

So let's twirl like the buds in a waltz,
Dodging the rain, avoiding the faults.
In this garden of laughter, let's frolic and sway,
With petals and giggles to brighten the day.

Bouquet of Whimsy

Gather 'round for a bouquet of fun,
Where daisies are silly and roses run.
With every stem, a tale is spun,
Of laughter and giggles, all in the sun.

A bunch of blooms with a colorful grin,
Whispering secrets, where do we begin?
The twisty tangle of leaves and stems,
Forms funky shapes like unkempt hems.

Petals prance like they own the floor,
With a hop and a leap, always wanting more.
Each flower's a joker, bursting with cheer,
Promising smiles from ear to ear.

So swing a bouquet, give it a whirl,
Toss petals like confetti and let laughter unfurl.
For in every bloom, there's a joke to share,
In this whimsical garden, all troubles repair.

Impressions of Indigo

In fields where colors play and dance,
A dandelion wore a fancy pants.
With hiccups of cheer and giggles so bright,
It wore a bowtie that sparkled in light.

The sun wore a hat, a comical sight,
While clouds gathered round for a jovial night.
The bees joined the party, buzzing in tune,
Sipping on nectar beneath the round moon.

Tall grass made jokes, tickling my toes,
While buttercups giggled, striking a pose.
Nature's own circus, a riotous spree,
Where laughter and petals dance wild and free.

So here's to the antics, the funny and bold,
Where laughter in gardens is a treasure to hold.
With ink of delight, let the verses spring,
For humor in flowers is a wonderful thing.

Footprints in the Flora

I tiptoed through petals, careful and shy,
But a ladybug winked as it zoomed by.
It said with a chuckle, 'What's the rush today?'
'Relax and enjoy,' it seemed to say.

A hedgehog in spectacles read me a book,
About mushrooms that danced, oh how they shook!
With each turn of page, I gasped and I laughed,
'Who knew mushrooms could waltz? They must be quite daft!'

The daisies stood proud with opinions to share,
Arguing loudly about who had the flair.
A butterfly swooped in, said, 'Calm down, dear friends!
Let's settle this quarrel; the fun never ends.'

So, I wandered through flora, each footstep a joke,
Where petals giggled and laughter awoke.
In nature's own comedy, I found my delight,
With footprints of laughter that sparkled so bright.

Nature's Tale

A squirrel in sunglasses stuck to a tree,
Called out to the flowers, 'Come party with me!'
The daisies replied with a nod and a grin,
'We'd love to, but first, let the wild dance begin!'

A caterpillar wiggled, wearing a crown,
Said, 'Join the parade! Don't let me down!'
The ants tapped their feet, ready to sway,
While the sunbeams chuckled, lighting the way.

A fish out of water, shouted with glee,
'The grass is so comfy, come sit next to me!'
But slipping and sliding, it flopped on the shore,
Leaving behind laughter and a giggle galore.

So listen to nature, it's telling a tale,
Of dancing and joy and the happy trail.
For in every corner where laughter prevails,
Are stories of friendship in Nature's grand scales.

The Poetry Patch

In a patch full of verses, much silly is grown,
With petals that rhyme in a whimsical tone.
The tulips tap dance while the violets sing,
Creating a melody, fluttering wing.

A fox in his waistcoat joins in the jam,
With rabbits in bowties, oh who gives a damn?
They sipped on the nectar of laughter and cheer,
Turning quiet gardens into a fun place to veer.

The sun made a joke, the clouds burst in laughter,
As squirrels wrote poems just for the crafter.
Dandelions floated, their fluff like confetti,
Celebrating words, oh what a delight they be!

So gather, dear friends, in this poetic space,
Where humor takes root and joy has its place.
For in this bright garden, with stories to hatch,
Life is a poem in the glorious patch.

Petal-Powered Lines

In gardens lush with giggles bright,
The flowers dance in pure delight.
With petals blushing, they declare,
"We've got jokes and puns to share!"

A dandelion cracks a smile,
While clovers chuckle all the while.
"What's green and loud? A talking pea!"
Oh, how they laugh, so joyfully!

The roses snicker, full of flair,
"Watch us twist and twirl in air!"
With every breeze, they sway and sway,
Making fun of clouds today.

Sprinkling laughter, what a sight,
In gardens filled with pure delight.
Their humor blooms, bright as the sun,
In this world of petal-powered fun!

Inked Blossoms

With ink that flows like morning dew,
The blossoms write just for you.
"Roses are red, violets are blue,
But have you smelled a tree? It's true!"

The daisies scribble silly lines,
"We're poets, kings of punchy rhymes!"
While sunflowers boast in grand display,
"Our verses shine, hip-hip-hooray!"

Tulips giggle in the breeze,
"We're blooming authors, if you please!"
With laughter echoing in the stay,
Their inked creations steal the day.

Each petal writes a tale untold,
With humor sweet, like honey gold.
So read their lines, let giggles flow,
In this garden of ink where fun will grow!

Rhyme Amongst the Roses

In a thicket where laughter grows,
You'll find some rhymes in rows and rows.
"Why did the flower bring a book?
To make the bees take a closer look!"

Each petal whispers cheeky thoughts,
Their rhymes are silly, but never fraught.
"What's a flower's favorite game?
Hide and seek! It's never the same!"

The tulips giggle, side by side,
"Join us on this fun-filled ride!"
With every quip, their joy unfurls,
In this garden, laughter twirls.

So come along, let's rhyme away,
With rosy giggles leading the way.
In a world where humor blooms and glows,
Join the fun amongst the rose!

Letters from the Lavender

A lavender patch sends out a cheer,
With letters filled with laughs so dear.
"Why did the bee get a bad grade?
It couldn't find its buzz, I'm afraid!"

With petals sweet, they pen their prose,
In purple hues where humor flows.
"Have you heard the joke about thyme?
It's a great herb, but can't keep time!"

Each letter drips with fragrant glee,
As bees gather, buzzing with glee.
"Write us back, don't let us wait,
We promise to send the best we create!"

In the garden where giggles thrive,
These lavender letters come alive.
With every note, they spread their bliss,
In a world where joy and fun exist!

Ephemeral Blossoms of Epiphany

In a garden where giggles sprout,
Every flower seems to shout,
"Pick me now! I'm at my best!"
But wilting soon, they need a rest.

Petals tickle the noses they greet,
As bees buzz around, oh what a treat!
A sunflower winks with a golden grin,
Saying, "Don't be shy, just jump right in!"

The daisies dance in a merry tightrope,
While butterflies whisper, "We'll dream of hope."
Yet soon the sun sets, the curtain will close,
Leaving us in soft, sweet, springtime prose.

A lily chuckles, "I'm only a tease,
One bright day, then I'm off with the breeze!"
Let's savor laughter in petals and dew,
Though the humor fades, we'll find something new!

Ink-Stained Garden Paths

In a place where words take root,
Where writers wander, boot by boot,
The pen that spills, an artist's dream,
Turns scribbles into a silly scheme.

A rose just giggled, it's painted blue,
"What of my color, who knew it's true?"
The inkpot spills in a chaotic swirl,
Making a mess, oh what a whirl!

A garden gnome chuckles, I must confess,
His hat's too big, what a funny mess!
While poems gather dust in the air,
The lilies shout, "We're beyond compare!"

As the sun dips low, the ink starts to dry,
We'll pen our thoughts with a wink and a sigh,
For in this patch of whimsical light,
Laughter blooms through the starry night.

Ballads of Blooms Unseen

When flowers sing in tones bizarre,
The tulips twirl beneath the star.
They whisper tales of what we miss,
In every laugh, there's a blooming kiss.

Petals plot, they scheme and conspire,
To distract us with their cheeky choir.
A dandy lion yells, "I'm the king!"
While purple pansies wear hats made of string.

Daisies laugh with a joyful cheer,
As bees band together to bring us near.
Over sticky honey, they share a tune,
That swirls like new blooms in full afternoon.

Yet twilight approaches, the party may end,
But off in the dark, new laughs will descend.
So raise a glass to the blooms out of sight,
For every night blooms a new jest and light!

The Opalescent Ink

With opalescent ink swirls so bright,
We scribble dreams into the night.
Each line a petal, each laugh a stem,
We weave our thoughts like a grand diadem.

A wink from the cosmos, a giggle from fate,
As dandelions whisper, "It's never too late!"
They float through the air on gossamer wings,
And all of a sudden, the heartstrings sing.

Sprinkling jokes like morning's dew,
With every petal, something new.
The colors burst in a riot of fun,
As laughter dances, it's never done.

So let's plunge our quills into laughter's drink,
Pour out the verses as thoughts interlink.
For in this garden of whimsical jest,
The opalescent ink will blossom the best!

Dreamscape of Blooms

In a garden of giggles, the flowers do play,
They wear silly hats and dance every day.
Bumblebees buzz with a comical grin,
As daisies tell jokes that make everyone spin.

The roses all gossip, their petals a-flutter,
While tulips make puns that are funny, not utter.
Underneath rainbows, the sunflowers spin,
Tickling the daisies, who can't help but grin.

In this whimsical place, the flowers are bright,
Chasing away shadows, bringing pure delight.
With a chuckle from nature, the blooms all unite,
Creating a world where silliness is right.

So come join the fun, let your worries take flight,
In a dreamscape of blooms, everything feels light.
Where laughter is nectar, and joy is the dew,
Together we'll blossom, just me and you.

Imagery in Indigo

A canvas of colors, with laughter in frames,
Indigo petals play silly little games.
They waltz with the wind, feet light as a feather,
Joking with clouds, oh—what a fine tether!

The violets laugh as the daffodils joke,
Spinning in circles like they're under a cloak.
With petals like smiles in shades of deep blue,
These whimsical blooms in a dance quite askew.

When rain starts to fall, they splash all around,
Finding new ways to turn up the sound.
In puddles they splash, creating a show,
Becoming little actors where laughter can flow.

So here in the garden, where humor takes root,
Every flower a jester, every leaf a hoot!
In imagery vivid, let everyone see,
The fun within flowers, where giggles run free!

The Scent of Stanzas

In a meadow of verses, where humor does bloom,
The stanzas are fragrant, dispelling all gloom.
With a whiff of a chuckle, the laughter ignites,
Turning each line into hilarious sights.

The tulips recite funny lines from their dreams,
While daisies declare that they're packing the creams.
They tickle the air with a poetic charm,
Wrapping giggles around us, a warmth in their arm.

As humor unfurls, the jokes take their flight,
In the scent of the stanzas, everything feels right.
Rosebuds sneak snickers, the lilies insist,
In our garden of laughter, there's no need to resist.

So come smell the laughter, it's fragrant and sweet,
With a pinch of delight, it's a grand little treat!
In this stanza-filled space, let your worries depart,
For the scent of the joyous lives deep in the heart.

Blooming Verses

In a patch of the quirky where nonsense prevails,
Blooming verses tumble like colorful tales.
With a pinch of wit in each petal that grows,
These flowers spin stories that tickle your toes.

The marigolds shout with a humorous cheer,
While orchids joke softly, "What's a flower's fear?"
A bouquet of laughter, all wrapped up with glee,
Blooming verses join in, as happy as can be.

Their roots intertwine, like punchlines in play,
Swaying to rhythms of a whimsical sway.
With every soft petal, there's joy in the air,
Where humor is woven in sunshine and care.

So let us all gather in this garden of jest,
Where blooming verses invite you to rest.
In laughter and color, let's dance without fears,
For the blooms tell their stories through chuckles and cheers!

The Garden Path of Words

In a garden where rhymes play,
The words waltz and sway.
They trip over roots so spry,
Laughing under the bright blue sky.

A dandelion jumped in glee,
Saying, "Come dance with me!"
A rose rolled its eyes, oh dear!
While the daisies chuckled near.

With every witty pun that grows,
The garden reflects what it shows.
A sunflower cracking a sharp joke,
As all the flowers laugh till they choke.

So wander paths of poetic delight,
Where petals shine in the morning light.
Embrace the humor that blooms so well,
In this whimsical garden where laughter dwells.

Echoing Blossoms

In a field where giggles thrive,
The blossoms come alive.
Each petal tells a tale so bright,
With whispers of joy and sheer delight.

"Why did the tulip cross the lane?"
To spread laughter, not just gain!
A butterfly stole the punchline quick,
Fluttering off with a cheeky trick.

Echoes of laughter bounce so free,
As daisies dance with glee.
They twist and turn in fuzzy hats,
Making light of silly spats.

In nature's stand-up, blooms unite,
Tickling each other until night.
For every flower knows it's true,
A hearty laugh brings joy anew.

Whispers in Lavender

In lavender fields, secrets bloom,
Where humor dispels any gloom.
Each humorist flower, quite absurd,
Shares jokes in whispers, never heard.

A bumblebee buzzed in on cue,
Saying, "I've got a joke for you!"
But tripped over a clover patch,
Wings flailing, a funny match!

The lavender giggles in the breeze,
As petals sway with playful tease.
Tales of pollen-thieves abound,
While butterflies chuckle all around.

So stroll through scents that twirl and tease,
And let the laughter float with ease.
For in this fragrant, joyful space,
Every whisper brings a smile to face.

Petals of Poetic Dreams

In a realm of dreams so bright,
Where petals prance in pure delight.
The poppies joke about the sun,
While daydreams wink, inviting fun.

A daffodil with a comical grin,
Said, "Let's see who can spin!"
But ended up in a tangled heap,
As the tulips laughed, "That's quite a leap!"

The daisies dropped their petals low,
Creating a stage for the show.
With every pun they wove in rhyme,
The air was filled with laughter's chime.

So gather 'round this garden dream,
Where petals dance and soft laughs beam.
In every bloom, a jest shines bright,
In this whimsical world of pure delight.

Secrets Beneath the Blooms

In gardens hid, a tale unfolds,
A bee named Lou, with secrets bold.
He buzzed around with a silly grin,
Whispering words that made flowers spin.

The roses blushed as they leaned near,
Listening close, they could barely hear.
With petals pink, they might take flight,
But all just giggled, it was pure delight.

Dandelions danced in the breezy air,
Their fluffy heads, a whimsical affair.
They tickled toes and spread such cheer,
What laughs they shared, all through the year!

So if you peek where blooms abound,
You'll find good humor in nature's sound.
With secrets kept beneath the green,
A funny world, so fresh and serene.

The Language of Indigo

In fields of blue, a chattering vine,
A chatting carrot, said, "Isn't life fine?"
With laughter ripe, they'd talk all day,
In indigo tones, they'd play their way.

A broccoli stalk jumped in too,
"Hey, did you hear the cabbage's view?"
They giggled loud, as green got wise,
The sun couldn't help but crack a smile.

On purple petals, a ladybug sat,
Telling puns that made all the plants chat.
"Why did the tomato blush?" she quipped,
"Because it saw the salad dressing, it flipped!"

So join in the fun, hear the laughter grow,
In shades of blue where silly seeds sow.
With every giggle under the sky,
The language of indigo flutters on by.

Echoes of Purple Prose

In a garden grand, where the wild things roam,
A prose-like parrot had made it his home.
He squawked of tales filled with quirky twists,
Winging words that danced like a jesting mist.

The flowers perked up, telling jokes so sweet,
"Why can't flowers stand up? Too many roots in their feet!"
The crowd erupted, petals all thrilled,
In laughter's embrace, the garden was filled.

An orchid joked, "I've a fantastic view,
But did you hear? My friend, the kale, breezed through!"
The daisies laughed, rolling in glee,
Echoes of purple prose wild and free.

So step into this world where humor shines bright,
In blooms and whispers, it feels just right.
Let echoes linger, as jokes never tire,
In this garden of prose fueled by laughter's fire.

Fragments of Floral Muse

Amidst the petals, a daffodil snickered,
"Do you smell something? Oh wait, it's my ticker!"
With every joke, the tulips would sway,
Fragments of laughter brightened their day.

A sunflower tilted, wearing a grin,
"I'm the brightest here, let the fun begin!"
The petals giggled, shades of pure cheer,
With humor blooming, there was nothing to fear.

A weed in disguise, spoke up with flair,
"Why don't you ever see me in despair?"
The roses all chuckled, petals aglow,
"We're all a bit crazy, but that's how we grow!"

So wander through this garden's sweet muse,
Where laughter replays, and joy you can't lose.
With fragments of fun that swirl on the breeze,
In nature's own rhythm, we laugh and appease.

www.ingramcontent.com/pod-product-compliance
Lightning Source LLC
Chambersburg PA
CBHW071820160426
43209CB00003B/141